# Time for a Field Trip

Nick Christopher

ROSEN COMMON CORE READERS

Rosen Classroom™

New York

Published in 2013 by The Rosen Publishing Group, Inc.
29 East 21st Street, New York, NY 10010



Book Design: Michael Harmon

Photo Credits: Cover Gallo Image/the Agency Collection/Getty Images; p. 4 Rich Reid/National Geographic/Getty Images; p. 5 Terence Mendoza/Shutterstock.com; p. 6 jakelv7500/Shutterstock.com; p. 7 Sergey Dubrov/Shutterstock.com; p. 8 Robert Asento/Shutterstock.com; p. 9 Evgeny Murtola/Shutterstock.com; p. 10 courtyardpix/Shutterstock.com; p. 11 Scruggelgreen/Shutterstock.com; p. 12 Nancy Kennedy/Shutterstock.com; p. 13 RonGreer.Com/Shutterstock.com; p. 14 Thomas Northcut/Digital Vision/Getty Images.

ISBN: 978-1-4488-8752-1
6-pack ISBN: 978-1-4488-8753-8

Manufactured in the United States of America

CPSIA Compliance Information: Batch #WS12RC: For further information contact Rosen Publishing, New York, New York at 1-800-237-9932.

Word Count: 134

# Contents

Today, my class is taking a field trip.
We're going to a farm!

First, we meet a farmer.
He cares for the plants and animals
on the farm.

The farmer shows us where the horses live.
Horses are beautiful animals.

I see ponies, too!

Ponies are small horses.

Then, we go to the barn.
We see spotted cows!
They have black spots.

Pigs live in the barn, too.
They have curly tails and pointy ears.

I see lots of plants on the farm!

I see colorful flowers.

I see apple trees.
They're a lot taller than I am!

We see lots of pumpkins!
We get pumpkins to take home.

My friend Jane finds a big pumpkin!
It's very heavy.

I like going on field trips with my class. The farm is a fun place!

# Making New Words

| | | |
|---|---|---|
| farm | → | farmer |
| beauty | → | beautiful |
| spot | → | spotted |
| curl | → | curly |
| point | → | pointy |
| color | → | colorful |
| tall | → | taller |

# Words to Know

spots

tails

# Index